Classroom Authoring: Guided Writing Grade 3

Editor
Kim Fields

Editorial Project Manager
Mara Ellen Guckian

Illustrator
Vicki Frazier

Cover Artist
Denise Bauer

Editors in Chief
Karen J. Goldfluss, M.S. Ed.
Ina Massler Levin, M.A.

Art Coordinator
Renée Christine Yates

Art Production Manager
Kevin Barnes

Creative Director
Karen J. Goldfluss, M.S. Ed.

Imaging
Rosa C. See
Ralph Olmedo, Jr.

Publisher
Mary D. Smith, M.S. Ed.

Author

Jima Dunigan, M.A.

Teacher Created Resources, Inc.
6421 Industry Way
Westminster, CA 92683
www.teachercreated.com

ISBN: 978-1-4206-3543-0

© 2008 Teacher Created Resources, Inc.
Made in U.S.A.

The classroom teacher may reproduce copies of materials in this book for classroom use only. Reproduction of any part for an entire school or school system is strictly prohibited. No part of this publication may be transmitted, stored, or recorded in any form without written permission from the publisher.

Table of Contents

Meeting Standards 3

Chapter 1: Guided Writing
Guiding Student Writers 5
Preparing the Students for Writing 7
Using the Powerful P's 8
    Step 1: Plan 8
    Step 2: Package 8
    Step 3: Pop 9
    Step 4: Polish 9
    Step 5: Publish 9
Writing Process 10
3-Point Scoring Rubric 12
Bloom's Taxonomy and the Writing Process . . 13
Powerful P's Mini Posters 14

Chapter 2: Vocabulary Development
Active Vocabulary Development 19
Sensory Vocabulary Chart 20
Writer's Vocabulary: Sensory Words 21
STAR Vocabulary 23
Transitional Words and Phrases 25
Synonyms 26
Synonym Webs 27
Word Clusters 28
Vivid Vocabulary
    Sports 29
    Winter 30

Chapter 3: Sentence Building
Teaching Sentence Building 31
Guided Sentence Building 32
Fixing Fragments 34
Simple Sentences 35
Compound Sentences 38
Statement Sentences 39
Question Sentences 40
Command Sentences 41
Exclamation Sentences 42

Chapter 4: Writing Paragraphs 43
6 Questions 44
    Fairy Tale 44
    My Sick Friend 46
    The Wishing Star 48
    Blank 6 Questions Form 50
COW Strategy 52
    Reptiles 54
    Shipwrecked 56
    My Garden 58
    Monster Sandwich 60
    Blank COW Strategy Form 62
Draw, Collect, Organize & Write 64
    My Room 64
    Blank Draw, Collect, Organize
    & Write Form 66

Chapter 5: Journaling
Introduction to Journaling 68
Daily Journaling 69
Character Journaling 70
Student-Teacher Journaling 71
Student-Parent Journaling 72
My Friend and I Journaling 73
Respond to Action 74

Chapter 6: Essays and Reports
Writing Essays and Reports 75
Sample Essay Writing Lesson
    Winter Fun 76
Essay Topics
    Spring 80
    Star Teacher 82
    Family Photo 84
    Fitness and Fun 86
    Transportation 88

Chapter 7:
Class Guided Writing 90
Story Planner 93
Blank Writing Page 95
Ideas for Story Writing 96

Meeting Standards

Each lesson in *Classroom Authoring: Guided Writing (Grade 3)* meets one or more of the following standards, which are used with permission from McRel. (Copyright 2000, McRel, Mid-continent Research for Education and Learning. Telephone: 303-337-0990 Website: www.mcrel.org.)

Language Arts Standards	Page Number
Uses the general skills and strategies of the writing process	
• Prewriting: Uses prewriting strategies to plan written work (e.g., discusses ideas with peers, draws pictures to generate ideas, writes key thoughts and questions, rehearses ideas, records reactions and observations)	8, 10–11, 13–14, 20, 24, 27–30, 44, 46, 48, 50, 54, 56, 58, 60, 62, 64, 66, 77, 80, 82, 84, 86, 88, 93
• Drafting and Revising: Uses strategies to draft and revise written work (e.g., rereads; rearranges words, sentences, and paragraphs to improve or clarify meaning; varies sentence type; adds descriptive words and details; deletes extraneous information; incorporates suggestions from peers and teachers; sharpens the focus)	8–11, 13, 15–16, 45, 47, 49, 51, 55, 57, 59, 61, 63, 65, 67, 79, 81, 83, 85, 87, 89, 94–95
• Editing and Publishing: Uses strategies to edit and publish written work (e.g., proofreads using a dictionary and other resources; edits for grammar, punctuation, capitalization, and spelling at a developmentally appropriate level; incorporates illustrations or photos; uses available appropriate technology to compose and publish work; shares finished product)	9–11, 13, 17–18, 45, 47, 49, 51, 55, 57, 59, 61, 63, 65, 67, 79, 81, 83, 85, 87, 89, 94–95
• Evaluates own and others' writing (e.g., asks questions and makes comments about writing, helps classmates apply grammatical and mechanical conventions)	9–11, 13, 17–18, 45, 47, 49, 51, 55, 57, 59, 61, 63, 65, 67, 79, 81, 83, 85, 87, 89, 94–95
• Uses strategies to organize written work (e.g., includes a beginning, middle, and ending; uses a sequence of events)	9–11, 13, 17–18, 45, 47, 49, 51, 55, 57, 59, 61, 63, 65, 67, 79, 81, 83, 85, 87, 89, 94–95
• Uses writing and other methods (e.g., using letters or phonetically spelled words, telling, dictating, making lists) to describe familiar persons, places, objects, or experiences	9–11, 13, 17–18, 45, 47, 49, 51, 55, 57, 59, 61, 63, 65, 67, 79, 81, 83, 85, 87, 89, 94–95
• Writes in a variety of forms or genres (e.g., picture books, friendly letters, stories, poems, information pieces, invitations, personal experiences, narratives, messages, responses to literature)	9–11, 13, 17–18, 45, 47, 49, 51, 55, 57, 59, 61, 63, 65, 67, 79, 81, 83, 85, 87, 89, 94–95
• Writes for different purposes (e.g., to entertain, inform, learn, communicate ideas)	9–11, 13, 17–18, 45, 47, 49, 51, 55, 57, 59, 61, 63, 65, 67, 79, 81, 83, 85, 87, 89, 94–95

Meeting Standards (cont.)

Language Arts Standards	Page Number
Uses the stylistic and rhetorical aspects of writing	
• Uses descriptive words to convey basic ideas	20–30
• Uses declarative and interrogative sentences in written compositions	33–42
Uses grammatical and mechanical conventions in written composition	
• Uses complete sentences in written compositions	33–42, 9–11, 13, 17–18, 45, 47, 49, 51, 55, 57, 59, 61, 63, 65, 67, 79, 81, 83, 85, 87, 89, 94–95
• Uses nouns in written compositions	33–42, 9–11, 13, 17–18, 45, 47, 49, 51, 55, 57, 59, 61, 63, 65, 67, 79, 81, 83, 85, 87, 89, 94–95
• Uses verbs in written compositions	33–42, 9–11, 13, 17–18, 45, 47, 49, 51, 55, 57, 59, 61, 63, 65, 67, 79, 81, 83, 85, 87, 89, 94–95
• Uses adjectives in written compositions	33–42, 9–11, 13, 17–18, 45, 47, 49, 51, 55, 57, 59, 61, 63, 65, 67, 79, 81, 83, 85, 87, 89, 94–95
• Uses adverbs in written compositions	33–42, 9–11, 13, 17–18, 45, 47, 49, 51, 55, 57, 59, 61, 63, 65, 67, 79, 81, 83, 85, 87, 89, 94–95
• Uses conventions of spelling in written compositions (e.g., spells high frequency, commonly misspelled words from appropriate grade level list; spells phonetically regular words; uses letter-sound relationships; spells basic short vowel, long vowel, r-controlled and consonant blend patterns, uses a dictionary and other resources to spell words)	9–11, 13, 17–18, 20–30, 33–42, 45, 47, 49, 51, 55, 57, 59, 61, 63, 65, 67, 79, 81, 83, 85, 87, 89, 94–95
• Uses conventions of capitalization in written compositions (e.g., first and last names, first word of a sentence)	9–11, 13, 17–18, 33–42, 45, 47, 49, 51, 55, 57, 59, 61, 63, 65, 67, 79, 81, 83, 85, 87, 89, 94–95
• Uses conventions of punctuation in written compositions (e.g., uses periods after declarative sentences, uses question marks after interrogative sentences, uses commas in a series of words)	9–11, 13, 17–18, 33–42, 45, 47, 49, 51, 55, 57, 59, 61, 63, 65, 67, 79, 81, 83, 85, 87, 89, 94–95

Chapter 1 — Guided Writing

Guiding Student Writers

Introduction to Guided Writing

Employing powerful techniques of guided instruction, this program replaces vague "writing experiences" with strong scaffolding needed for the students to learn, master, and enjoy writing. *Classroom Authoring: Guided Writing (Grade 3)* is packed with specific help for the teacher and a rich supply of student activities in vocabulary and sentence building and paragraph and story writing. Following this program will result in your students becoming strong, confident writers. The students will become independent writers as they internalize organizational strategies and writing process steps during their guided writing experiences. Guided writing provides the support for success while the students learn to write.

Guiding Student Writers

Teachers must teach students with diverse experiences and abilities. Most third graders come into the classroom reading and writing for various purposes. Others need extensive instruction and vocabulary development. Additionally, the students must write more detailed and descriptive passages. Finally, students must think about what to write, organization, vocabulary, spelling, grammar, and punctuation rules. All must be addressed.

Not so long ago, a writing lesson meant the teacher made an assignment, and the student did the best he or she could with no guidance. Then the teacher had to correct the errors, suggest reorganization, and mold the final product. Now, we know so much more about the art and science of writing. By being proactive with organization, practicing modeled and guided writing while leading the students through the writing process, and introducing powerful strategies, we now teach writing instead of simply making assignments. *Classroom Authoring: Guided Writing (Grade 3)* features a guided writing method, sequential writing process, and a variety of strategies to make teaching writing simple for the teacher and learning writing skills an enjoyable process for the students.

Guiding Student Writers (cont.)

Timing

Do not allow the students to go ahead of or lag behind the class during the crucial first few attempts to use a certain writing strategy. Teach the class to remain quiet while others finish a sentence or a section. Noise and distractions can divert students from the task and slow the process.

Once instructions for a sentence or section are clear, tell the class how much time is left for that portion. Say, "You have 90 seconds to write the sentence responding to idea one on the list." The students will soon understand that working quickly is important and that completing the task is a requirement. When time is up, ask, "Who needs 30 more seconds?" Teach the students to respond silently by raising a hand and quickly getting back to work. After each class member has completed that sentence, the teacher asks for two or three students to volunteer to share their sentences. This gives an opportunity for the students to share their writing with the class and get quality, positive feedback from the teacher.

Invented Spelling

Always use correct spellings when modeling a lesson. Discuss how a word could be spelled and how it should be spelled. The word *phone* sounds like /f/ /ō/ /n/ but is spelled *p, h, o, n, e*. When a student worries about spelling, the writing process comes to a halt. Say, "Spell the word like it sounds. We will repair spelling together later during conferencing. I will not be disappointed as long as you try."

Withdrawing Support

After the students have had several writing assignments using a strategy, the teacher will continue to facilitate discussions one sentence at a time. However, the students will write individual sentences on their own papers. All the students will be writing about the same idea from the graphic organizer at the same time, but their individual responses will be different.

As the students gain independence in the strategy, give less and less support. *The goal of guided writing is for the students to become independent writers.*

Chapter 1 — *Guided Writing*

Preparing the Students for Writing

Materials (for the teacher to model writing)
- overhead projector and transparency sheets (whiteboard/chart paper/data projector/computer)
- fine-point transparency markers or markers to write on whiteboard/chart paper
- hanging file to store transparencies to return to same idea during next writing session

Materials (for each student)
- three-ring binder
- clear plastic sleeves for word lists
- zippered pencil pouch and several sharpened pencils
- paper
- specific storage area for binder
- hanging file in filing cabinet for finished work

Modeling Guided Writing Strategies

In the **Guided Writing Method**, the teacher plays an interactive role as he or she guides the students through each step of the writing process while incorporating various strategies. A **Guided Writing Strategy** is a specific approach used to accomplish a task. For example, STAR is a vocabulary development strategy used prior to writing about a topic (see pages 23–24). The COW strategy helps the students develop a complete paragraph (see pages 52–53).

During modeling, the teacher will *think aloud* (talk aloud about how and what he or she is thinking). First, the teacher will think aloud about the prompt or writing assignment. He or she will ask questions aloud about what the prompt requires him or her to do and talk through the process of coming up with answers. The students will hear the teacher as he or she thinks aloud and makes decisions. Next, the teacher will think aloud as he or she decides on a graphic organizer and draws it for the students to see. Then, the teacher will generate ideas or ask for student ideas and record them on the graphic organizer.

Note: During modeling the students may participate orally, but they may not write.

Think-Aloud Example

The teacher gives the prompt, "Tigers." The teacher or a student contributes an idea such as "tigers are felines." The teacher will think aloud for the students to hear as he or she decides to add the idea to the organizer or leave it out. The teacher will think aloud, "Does the idea, 'tigers are felines' fit with the idea of writing about tigers? Yes, tigers are from the feline family, so it goes with the big idea, 'Tigers.'" If a student suggests, "My kitten is named Tiger," the teacher will think aloud, "My kitten is named Tiger may be a true statement, but it does not tell me anything about the main topic, tigers. That idea does not belong, so I will leave it out."

After that, the teacher models think-aloud as he or she decides on the sequence for the ideas. (You may number the words or make a new list to arrange the ideas in order.) Once the ideas are organized, the teacher will complete the activity by doing think alouds to create individual sentences about the ideas on the list and writing them for the students to see. The teacher can engage students by asking for sentence ideas. As the students decide on sentences, the teacher writes them for the class to see. He or she will have opportunities to discuss capital letters, end punctuation, subjects and verbs, and spelling.

Chapter 1 *Guided Writing*

Using the Powerful P's

The **Guided Writing Process** is a step-by-step recipe for writing that includes planning, writing, editing, revising, and publishing. In *Classroom Authoring: Guided Writing (Grade 3)*, the students use five Powerful P's: Plan, Package, Pop, Polish, and Publish. Use the steps below to model the Guided Writing Process. Each step the teacher completes is marked with a T. Each step the student completes is designated by an S. The Powerful P Mini Posters (pages 14–18) can be enlarged and displayed to remind the students about each step of the process and what they need to do in each step. The Writing Process chart on pages 10–11 is a quick reference tool for the teacher to see what he or she needs to do during each step.

Step 1: Plan

The teacher (T) models a think-aloud activity. Then the students (S) write along with the teacher to develop a plan for their writing projects.

Description of Steps

(T) 1. Provide the writing prompt for the project.

(T) 2. Guide the think-aloud: What type of writing will the students be doing (e.g., poem, story)? Who is the audience for the project (e.g., peers, U.S. president)?

(T)(S) 3. Select and draw a graphic organizer.

(T)(S) 4. Collect ideas for the writing project.

(T)(S) 5. Collect words using a Guided Writing Strategy (e.g., STAR [page 23], COW [page 52]).

(T)(S) 6. Record ideas and words on the graphic organizer.

(T)(S) 7. Arrange the ideas in sequential order. (You may have the students number the ideas or mark each as beginning, middle, or end.)

(T) 8. Establish a rubric assessment tool for the students (see page 12). Tell the students which criteria you will be focusing on for this assignment. (Always teach toward the highest score on the rubric.)

Step 2: Package

The teacher guides the students in a write-along as they follow the plan to write their first draft—one sentence at a time.

Description of Steps

(T)(S) 1. Examine the idea sequence. (See Step 1: Plan, #7 above.)

(S) 2. Make sentence suggestions for the writing project.

(T) 3. Help the students decide on the best sentences to use for the project.

(T)(S) 4. Write each sentence (e.g., introduction, details, conclusion).

(T) 5. Use opportunities during the write-along to discuss spelling, mechanics, word choice, and sentence structure.

Chapter 1 Guided Writing

Using the Powerful P's *(cont.)*

Step 3: Pop

Using the established rubric, the teacher and individual students conference on paragraphs—popping ideas and words in, out, and/or around.

- (T) 1. Discuss only one point with the student at a time, giving suggestions for improvements.
- (T) 2. Give one positive comment.
- (S) 3. Rewrite first draft, making improvements. Refer to a word list (e.g., pages 21–22) to *pop in* details and words that fit the project. *Pop out* repetitions and unnecessary words or phrases. *Pop around* ideas and words so that the sentences make sense. (The students may erase/rewrite on the first draft or use a red pen to write on top of the draft.)
- (T)(S) 4. Repeat Steps 1–3 until the student has made a specific number of improvements to the draft.

Step 4: Polish

The students polish their writing projects, with assistance as needed, to compose a final draft.

- (S) 1. Check each sentence for a capital letter and end mark.
- (T)(S) 2. Check spellings with assistance of a beginning dictionary, friend, spell check, or teacher conference.
- (T) 3. Instruct the student to write a final neat copy after approval of changes to the draft.
- (T) 4. Use the rubric assessment tool (introduced in Step 1: Plan, #8) to score one criteria per writing project.

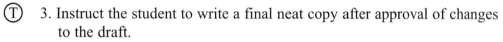
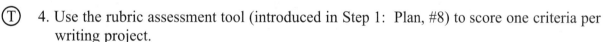

Step 5: Publish

The students share their completed work and celebrate their accomplishment.

- (T)(S) 1. Congratulate the students on their completion of the writing project.
- (S) 2. Select and complete one or more of the following ideas:
    a. Share your project with friends.
    b. Read your writing to the class or your family.
    c. Display your project on the wall.
    d. Print your writing in the school newsletter, a class book, or other format.
    e. Place your project in a portfolio, binder, notebook, or scrapbook.
    f. Send your writing to a friend, relative, or the mayor.

Writing Process

Powerful P's	What Teachers and Students Do	How Teachers Guide Writing
Prepare Students Model examples.	**Teacher models a writing strategy using think-aloud while students contribute orally. Students do not write.** • Teacher models making a graphic organizer for the strategy • Teacher models collecting ideas (from units, basal) • Teacher models organizing ideas in a sequence • Teacher models writing introductory and detail sentences	**Prepare students by building background knowledge and modeling examples of strategies.** • Model using graphic organizer of the strategy • Model idea collecting • Model sequence planning • Model writing sentences using sequence plan
Plan Identify the task; collect and organize the ideas.	**Teacher models and guides writing. Students write along.** • Teacher guides analyzing prompt and identifying • Teacher guides drawing a graphic organizer • Teacher guides creating vocabulary lists and collecting ideas • Teacher guides organizing ideas in a sequence • Teacher provides or helps plan rubric	**Plan lessons with the end in mind: plan each step.** • Plan the prompt • Plan and use graphic organizer • Plan and use vocabulary/idea collection strategy • Require sequencing of ideas • Plan rubric to guide conferences and assessment
Package Teacher guides the writing.	**Teacher guides and writes. Students write along.** • Teacher facilitates students in developing a class introductory sentence; teacher writes for all to see; students write along • Teacher guides students in developing detail sentences; teacher writes for all to see; students write along • Teacher keeps all students on same idea and same sentence using timing techniques	**Give instructions in small bites.** • Decriminalize spelling—when students are writing, thoughts should flow freely; repair spelling last • Stay involved—writing is interactive • Keep students on track; use timing techniques to motivate

Chapter 1 *Guided Writing*

Writing Process *(cont.)*

Powerful P's	What Teachers and Students Do	How Teachers Guide Writing
Pop Revive—pop ideas or words in, out, or around	**Conference and give feedback. Students use red pens.** • Conference with each student; give praise • Students erase and rewrite or overwrite with red pens • Pop ideas: STAR vocabulary in, words out, change words around	**Give positive feedback.** • Hold brief individual conferences (about 30 seconds) • Require a certain number of improvements • Use rubric to guide conferences
Polish Edit—check over everything and write a neat copy	**Conference and give feedback. Students use red pens.** • Check spelling (teacher, friend, dictionary) • Check punctuation, capitalization (self, teacher, friend) • Write a neat copy	**Give feedback on students' progress.** • Help students polish spellings • Help students check punctuation and capitalization • Use rubric to judge completed work
Publish Share with others.	**Students share!** • Read aloud project in class, post on the wall, read to friends or family, send to relative, keep a portfolio . . . Celebrate!	**Praise students' accomplishments.** • Facilitate sharing of students' work
Practice	**Teacher and student go through the process again using a new prompt.** • Teacher gradually releases responsibility	**Facilitate students' repeating of writing process.** • Growth takes time, gradually release responsibility to student

©Teacher Created Resources, Inc. 11 #3543 *Classroom Authoring Guided Writing*

3-Point Scoring Rubric

	STRUCTURE	SUPPORTING DETAILS	SENTENCES	VOCABULARY	CONVENTIONS of ENGLISH LANGUAGE	CREATIVITY/ VOICE
3	**Quality Structure** • Indented • Logical order • Beginning, middle, ending • Good transitions • Attention getter	**Quality Support** • Strong use of details • Stayed on topic • Eight or more support sentences	**Quality Sentences** • Complete sentences • Sentence variety: three or more simple, compound, complex, statement, question, command, exclamatory	**Quality Vocabulary** • Adjectives • Adverbs • Precise word choice	**Quality Conventions** Few errors: • Punctuation • Capitalization • Precise use of phonics spellings with conventional spellings	**Quality Creativity** • Quality items • Quality descriptions • Quality approach • Purpose accomplished
2	**Good Structure** • Some logic • May lack beginning, middle, or ending • May lack transitions	**Good Support** • Some examples • Some focus • Six or more support sentences	**Good Sentences** • May contain minor errors • May lack sentence variety	**Good Vocabulary** • Adjectives • Adverbs • Simple words	**Good Conventions** Some errors: • Punctuation • Capitalization • Precise use of phonics spellings with conventional spellings	**Good Creativity** • Quality items • Quality descriptions • Quality approach • Purpose accomplished
1	**Beginner Structure** • Lacking logic • No beginning, middle, or ending • No transitions • Difficult to follow	**Beginner Support** • Limited examples • Unclear • Four or fewer support sentences	**Beginner Sentences** • Run-on sentences • Fragments	**Beginner Vocabulary** • Rambling • Repetitive • Incorrect words • Inadequate	**Beginner Conventions** Many errors: • Punctuation • Capitalization • Poor phonics spellings	**Beginner Creativity** • No apparent theme • Limited descriptions • Purpose not accomplished
0	**No Paragraph Characteristics** • No structure • No sentences • May have words	**No Development** • No examples • No focus • No support sentences	**No Sentences** • Incomplete sentences • Few words	**Limited Vocabulary** • Difficult to understand • Illegible • Few words	**No Conventions** Many errors: • No punctuation • No capitalization • Gross misspellings • Illegible	**No Creativity** • No apparent theme • No descriptions • Purpose not accomplished

Bloom's Taxonomy and the Writing Process

Bloom's Taxonomy has been revised. The most notable differences are changing the terms from nouns to verbs and the rearranging and/or renaming of the six levels. Create has been added as the highest order in thinking. Bloom's Taxonomy applies to each stage of the writing process; the chart below aligns Bloom's Taxonomy with the writing process levels and gives suggested terms to use when the teacher talks to the students about writing.

Bloom's Taxonomy	Writing Process Powerful P's	Language to Use During Writing Lessons							
Remember (was Knowledge)	Plan	cluster	describe	identify	locate	omit	record	select	
		collect	discuss	label	name	outline	recount	sort	
		define	find	list	observe	recall	retell		
Understand (was Comprehend)	Plan	cite	determine	document	extend	predict	report	review	
		classify	display	explain	infer	prove	represent	summarize	
		demonstrate	distinguish	express	match	recognize	restate	support	
Apply	Plan, Package	act	calculate	compute	dramatize	exhibit	imagine	show	
		apply	categorize	count	draw	generalize	imitate	solve	
		build	choose	draft	execute	illustrate	sequence		
Analyze	Pop	ask	compare	debate	differentiate	map	question		
	Polish	break down	connect	decide	examine	order	relate		
		check	contrast	defend	interpret	organize	research		
Evaluate (used to be highest level)	Pop, Polish, Publish	assess	critique	judge	rank	test			
		conclude	grade	prioritize	score				
Create (replaces Evaluate as highest level)	All Five P's	combine	construct	explain	generate	produce			
		compose	design	formulate	invent	respond			

Powerful P's—Step 1: Plan

1. What am I writing?
   (story, poem, letter)

2. Who is my reader?
   (friends, family, mayor)

3. How will I do it?
   (Choose and draw a graphic organizer.)

4. What do I need?
   (Use a strategy to collect ideas and words.)

5. Put ideas in order.
   (beginning, middle, ending)

Powerful P's—Step 2: Package

1. Follow the idea plan.

2. Write the introduction sentence.

3. Write the detail sentences.

4. Write the concluding sentence.

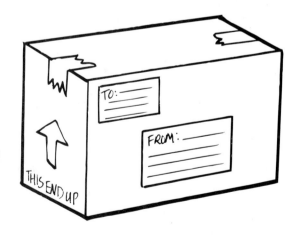

Powerful P's—Step 3: Pop

- **Should I pop words or ideas in? (Add details.)**

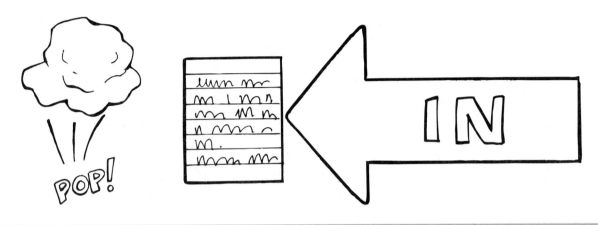

- **Should I pop words or ideas out? (Erase/rewrite to delete repetition and unnecessary words/phrases.)**

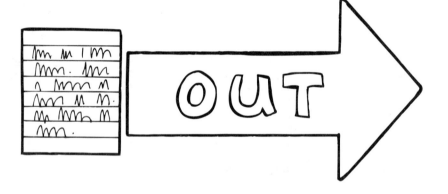

- **Should I pop words or ideas around? (Change order for clarity.)**

Powerful P's—Step 4: Polish

1. Check each sentence for a capital letter and end mark.

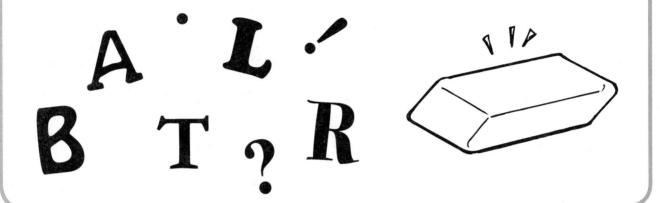

2. Check for spelling.

3. Write a neat final copy.

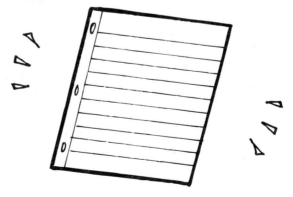

Powerful P's—Step 5: Publish

- **Share your project with friends.**
- **Read your writing to the class or your family.**

- **Display your project on the wall.**
- **Print your writing in the school newsletter, a class book, or other format.**

- **Place your project in a portfolio, binder, notebook, or scrapbook.**
- **Send your writing to a friend, relative, or the mayor.**

Chapter 2   *Vocabulary Development*

Active Vocabulary Development

Vocabulary should be part of every plan for writing. Vocabulary instruction and collection as prewriting strategies directly affect the quality of the finished writing product.

Vocabulary development has four levels: listening, speaking, reading, and writing. Writing vocabulary is the slowest to develop. The students automatically develop writing vocabulary if they are actively and frequently engaged in writing, but they may not be aware of it. They will benefit from direct instruction in writing vocabulary by learning categories of words, including sensory vocabulary (pages 20–22), STAR vocabulary (pages 23–24), transitional words and phrases (page 25), synonyms (pages 26–27), word clusters (page 28), and thematic vocabulary (pages 29–30).

Using ideas from this chapter, the teacher can gradually build word banks (e.g., word walls, student word reference sheets) as the students acquire words. As words are added, tell the students that these words are essential for writers to know and use.

Writer's Vocabulary

Third grade students will develop writing vocabulary during the first part of the year. To facilitate the development of a writing vocabulary, the teacher should begin making word banks. Try using the categories on pages 21–22. Around the middle of third grade, provide the students with these lists to store in their binders as references for spelling.

STAR Vocabulary

STAR stands for **S**ensory, **T**echnical, **A**ctive, and **R**eal Talk vocabulary words. This acronym helps the students remember to collect vocabulary from a variety of sources in preparation for writing. After the teacher establishes a topic for writing, the students are guided to brainstorm vocabulary related to that topic, which also fits under a STAR vocabulary category (see pages 23–24).

Transitional Words and Phrases

Transitional vocabulary assists organization and provides flow to written work. Transitional words and phrases show how ideas are related. The relationships may be based on concepts such as time, space, or comparison (see page 25).

Along with the students, the teacher should create word bank categories for transitional words and phrases. Develop these lists over time as the students acquire them in content vocabulary.

Thematic Vocabulary

Vocabulary development in this text will focus mainly on categories of words (see Vivid Vocabulary on pages 29–30 for samples of word categories). However, word study in any of the forms below increases overall word knowledge:

• affixes	• compound words	• onsets	• homographs
• antonyms	• prefixes	• 50-cent words	• rimes
• word families	• homonyms	• suffixes	• rhymes

Chapter 2   Vocabulary Development

Sensory Vocabulary Chart

Help your students practice developing sensory vocabulary using the blank chart below, or create your own on an overhead transparency for the students to see. Select a topic and guide the class to collect words for each column. (See the example below.) Motion words refer to the sensation of movement. Emotion words are also sensory because emotions are felt or sensed. Not all categories will have entries in the columns.

<u>Swimming in a Pond</u>
Subject

See	Hear	Touch	Smell & Taste	Motion	Emotion
water	splashing	damp	pond smell	diving	fear
fish	laughing	cold	fish smell	floating	excitement
frogs	shouts	fish		running	happiness
insects		slimy			joy
rocks		slick			fun
logs					

_____
Subject

See	Hear	Touch	Smell & Taste	Motion	Emotion

Writer's Vocabulary: Sensory Words

Sight Words			Sound Words		
Appearance	Color	Movement	Loud Sounds	Soft Sounds	Voice Sounds
bent	aqua	bounce	bang	buzz	bark
brilliant	beige	crawl	blaring	chime	chant
clear	black	creep	boom	chirp	chatter
dazzling	blue	curl	clash	clink	cheer
dull	brass	dart	crack	groan	chuckle
faded	bronze	dash	crash	grunt	cluck
flat	dark	dive	deafening	gurgle	coo
freckled	emerald	drift	echo	hum	cry
fresh	gold	drive	grate	jingle	giggle
giant	green	flip	howl	moan	growl
gigantic	light	gallop	jangle	mumble	guffaw
jagged	lime	nod	knock	murmur	gurgle
lumpy	mauve	poke	pop	mutter	hiss
messy	navy	scramble	racket	patter	howl
misty	orange	sneak	rap	peep	laugh
mound	pastel	sprint	roar	rustle	puff
muddy	pearl	stroll	rumble	sigh	raspy
opaque	purple	swoop	scream	swish	scratchy
round	red	trot	screech	tinkle	sing
shabby	silver	twirl	slam	twitter	snicker
shiny	teal	wade	squawk	whimper	snort
squiggly	tone	wiggle	thud	whine	stammer
striped	turquoise	yawn	wail	whir	throaty
twinkle	white	zip	whoop	whisper	trill
wavy	yellow	zoom	yell	whistle	yodel

Writer's Vocabulary: Sensory Words (cont.)

Touch, Taste, Smell Words			Feelings Words		
Touch	**Taste**	**Smell**	**Anger**	**Happy**	**Fear**
brittle	acidic	aroma	agitated	adore	afraid
bumpy	appetizing	cheesy	boil	affection	alarm
crisp	bitter	coffee	bristle	animated	anxious
damp	bland	cologne	burst	bouncy	concern
dusty	burnt	fragrant	explode	cheerful	cowardly
furry	buttery	foul	fierce	chipper	dismay
fuzzy	fishy	fresh	fume	content	dread
glossy	fruity	garlic	fury	delighted	faint
gritty	luscious	mild	hostile	elated	fright
icy	meaty	moldy	infuriate	festive	horror
jelly	mouthwatering	musty	irate	hug	nervous
leathery	nutty	odor	mad	joyful	nightmare
mushy	rotten	onion	rage	kind	panic
oily	salty	perfume	reckless	merry	quaking
rocky	savory	pleasant	seethe	peppy	shaky
silky	scrumptious	rancid	steamed	pleased	shocking
slick	smoky	reek	stomp	satisfied	skittish
slimy	sour	rotten	upset	share	terror
slippery	spicy	scent	wild	sunny	timid
smooth	spoiled	sharp	wrath	tickled	worried
soaked	sweet	sniff			
solid	tangy	sour			
spongy	tart	stinky			
sticky	tasteless	sweet			
warm	yummy	whiff			

Chapter 2 *Vocabulary Development*

STAR Vocabulary

Make four columns on the board, overhead, or chart paper. Write the headings *Sensory, Technical, Active,* and *Real Talk* at the head of the columns.

Based on a specific topic, guide the students to develop a list of **sensory** words for the Sensory column. The sensory vocabulary includes see, hear, taste, touch, smell, motion, and emotion words. Then, help the students generate a list of **technical** terms relevant to the topic for the Technical column. For example, technical vocabulary for a story about a zoo might include *veterinarian* and *zookeeper.* Next, help the students realize that writing needs active voice by creating a list of **active** movement words in the Active column. After that, guide the students to write phrases that characters in that story genre might say. Record these in the Real Talk section. Some words will overlap columns; those words are probably the best choices to use in the paragraph, story, or essay.

Trip to the Zoo			
Sensory Words	**Technical Words**	**Active Words**	**Real Talk**
animal sounds aviary crowds elephants hay hot sun laughter	carnivore diet habitat safari veterinarian zookeeper	feeding climbing flying screeching sightseeing taking pictures trumpeting	"Look at that tropical bird." "Don't feed the animals!" "Let's go to the panda exhibit next."

Demonstrate that STAR vocabulary lists can be made anywhere—on the board, an overhead transparency, blank sheets of paper, or poster boards. At first, the students will need the STAR Vocabulary sheet on page 24. As the students assimilate the idea of STAR vocabulary, they may no longer need the form but will be able to create appropriate lists on their own.

Encourage the students to include STAR vocabulary terms in their first draft. After finishing the draft, have each student compare his or her draft with the list again and try to fit in more vocabulary as appropriate. Pumping up vocabulary improves the quality of writing!

Note: Type and copy lists for the students to keep in their binders. These word lists will be resources for future writing.

STAR Vocabulary

Name _____ Date _____

Subject _____

Real Talk	Active	Technical	Sensory

Transitional Words and Phrases

Time Order Words

after	finally	next	third
already	first	once	tomorrow
always	last	second	until
at the same time	later	soon	yesterday
before	long ago	since	
during	meanwhile	suddenly	
earlier	never	then	

Spatial Order Words

above	farthest	near	overlap
around	highest	nearest	surround
behind	in back of	next to	under
below	in front of	on the left	underneath
beside	in the middle	on the right	
border	inside	outside	
circle	lowest	over	

Comparison Words

bad	good	small	sweeter
best	least	smaller	weak
better	less	smallest	weaker
big	milder	spicier	weakest
bigger	more	strong	worse
biggest	most	stronger	worst
equal	same	strongest	

Cause and Effect Words

as a result	consequently	for this reason	since
because	due to	if . . . then	so

Chapter 2   Vocabulary Development

Synonyms

Draw a large circle in the middle of a sheet of chart paper and write a word in the circle that has many synonyms. (A *synonym* is one of two or more words that have the same or nearly the same meaning.) Draw lines out from the circle to create a synonym web. Guide the students to contribute other words that mean the same. Display the chart in a classroom word bank (word wall, chart, student reference sheet) to encourage the students to use synonyms in their writing. Make a copy of the Synonym Reference Chart (below) for students to put in their binders.

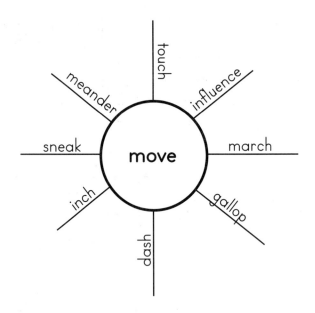

Synonym Reference Chart

Word	Synonyms
big	huge, enormous, gigantic, giant
little	minute, tiny, wee, petite
great	tremendous, awesome, fantastic, wonderful
happy	joyous, pleased, content, amused
sad	distressed, upset, unhappy, blue
pretty	lovely, attractive, gorgeous, beautiful
like	adore, enjoy, favor, fancy
know	learn, discover, believe
let	allow, approve, permit, tolerate
walk	saunter, stroll, amble, hike
run	gallop, dash, race, zip
look	glance, stare, peek, peer
said	replied, stated, exclaimed, moaned
say	whisper, state, exclaim, mention

Chapter 2 Vocabulary Development

Name _____ Date _____

Synonym Webs

Write words on the first web that mean the same or nearly the same as the word *eat*. Then complete the second synonym web for the word *sleep*.

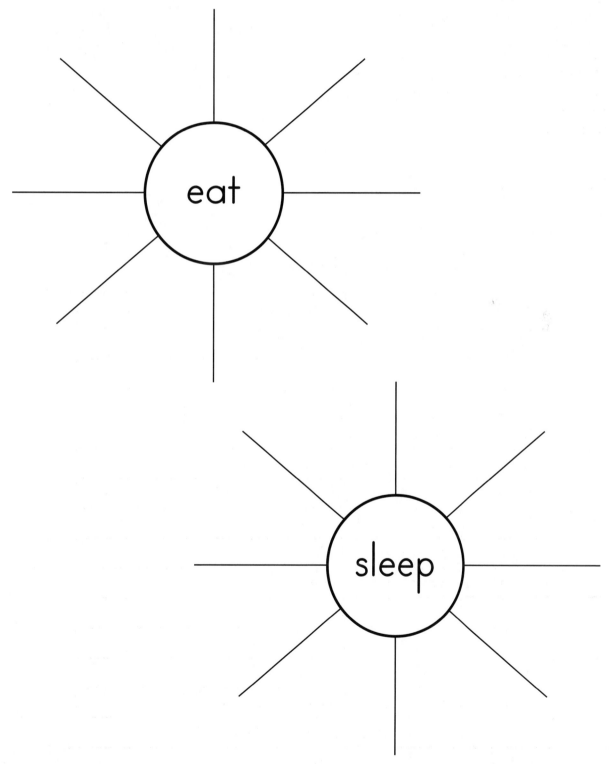

Chapter 2 Vocabulary Development

Name_____ Date_____

Word Clusters

Begin with the word your teacher gives you and write it in the center of the star. Follow the directions on the other shapes to make associations to the given word.

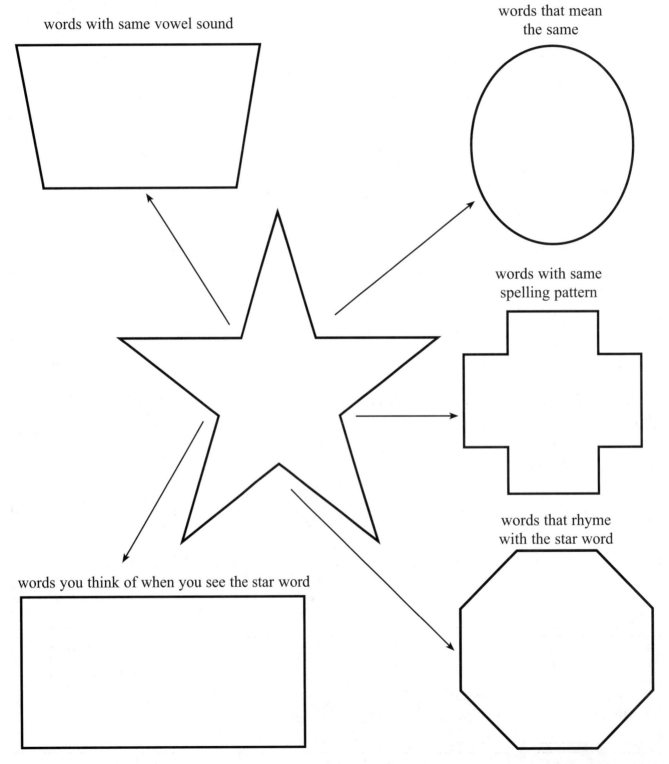

Chapter 2 — Vocabulary Development

Name _____   Date _____

Vivid Vocabulary
Sports

Try to find a word for each letter of the alphabet that is sports-related. Write each word in the corresponding box. Some words have already been provided. (You may work alone, in small groups, or as a class.)

A	G	M	S
All Stars announcer _____	glove grand slam goalie guard _____	Major League mitt mouthpiece _____	score second base shoot sideline slam dunk soccer stadium Stanley Cup steal strike Super Bowl
B baseball bleachers basketball block batter bunt _____	**H** halftime home run helmet home plate hockey stick _____	**N** net _____	
C catcher coach centerfield curve ball cleats _____	**I** inning intercept _____	**O** offense outfield _____	**T** time out touchdown tight end tournament third base turnover
D defense dribble diamond dugout down _____	**J** jersey _____	**P** pass pop fly pitcher puck player _____	**U** umpire uniform _____
E error _____	**K** kicker _____	**Q** quarter quarterback _____	**V** volley _____
			W walk World Cup whistle World Series
F face mask football free throw _____	**L** layup leather line backer _____	**R** rebound referee receiver rink _____	**X Y Z** zone

Chapter 2 Vocabulary Development

Name _____ Date _____

Vivid Vocabulary

Winter

Try to find a word for each letter of the alphabet that is related to winter. Write each word in the corresponding box. Some words have already been provided. (You may work alone, in small groups, or as a class.)

A Alaska Arctic Antarctica avalanche _____	**G** gale-force gifts glacier gloves Greenland greeting card grizzly bear _____	**J** Jack Frost _____	**R** reindeer ribbon roasted marshmallows _____
B black ice blubber blizzard bobsled boots _____		**K** knit _____	**S** scarf shovel skis sled sleet snowboard snowstorm sweater _____
	H harness hockey holiday hooves hot cocoa hunt huskies _____	**L** lantern logs Lapps _____	
C cabin camping stove Canada _____		**M** mittens moose mountains _____	
			T thaw _____
D dogsled drift _____		**N** New Year's Eve Northern Lights _____	
	I iceberg ice fishing ice skates ice storm icicle icy Iditarod igloo insulate Inuit		**U** _____
E earmuffs elk evergreens _____		**O** _____	**V** _____
		P parka polar bear pine presents plow _____	
F firewood fort flannel freeze fleece frigid floe frost flurry frozen foggy fuel _____			**W** wind chill wool _____
		Q quilt _____	**X Y Z** _____

Teaching Sentence Building

Introduction to Sentence Building

Young writers will gain knowledge and experience about sentence writing from continued practice and application. While the students write sentences, the teacher should reinforce good grammar, punctuation, and sentence structure. Although it is important to study sentence structure and development, the students will also gain experience in sentence writing from using the activities in Chapter 4 (Writing Paragraphs), Chapter 5 (Journaling), Chapter 6 (Essays and Reports), and Chapter 7 (Story Writing).

Guided Sentence Building

Make transparency copies of Guided Sentence Building (pages 32–33). Using page 32 on the overhead, show the students how to build a descriptive sentence. Then guide the students through page 33. Begin with two words—a subject and a predicate. Ask the students to tell more about the subject. Write the description on the line below the subject. Ask for more information about the predicate and write it on the line below. Keep the line that separates the subject and predicate to help the students understand that they are adding meaning to the subject or the predicate. By adding words or phrases to the subject or predicate, the writer makes the sentence more interesting and meaningful for the reader.

After several practice sessions using the Guided Sentence Building form (page 33), direct the students to draw their own building sentences frames and guide them in the process. The students will soon be able to do this activity independently.

Fixing Fragments

Have the students read *Mufaro's Beautiful Daughters* by John Steptoe. Then instruct them to use sentence parts taken from the tale to write new, complete sentences on page 34. (Sentences do not have to match the sentences in the book.)

Writing a Variety of Sentences

The students will learn how to write simple and compound sentences and use conjunctions (see pages 35–38). The students need to be taught how to vary sentence beginnings. Teach the use of conjunctions *(and, or, but)* to connect two simple sentences.

It is important for young writers to understand that there are statement, question, command, and exclamation sentences. Pages 39–42 give the students an opportunity to practice forming each type of sentence.

Guided Sentence Building

Subject	Predicate
Dakota	ran.
Dakota Trent	ran swiftly.
Dakota Trent on the Polar team	ran swiftly toward the end zone.
Dakota Trent on the Polar team	ran carefully and swiftly toward the end zone.

Chapter 3 · Sentence Building

Name _____ Date _____

Guided Sentence Building

Write a single subject and a single predicate using a capital letter and end mark. On the following lines, add more information to the subject and the predicate to improve and build each sentence.

Subject	Predicate

Subject	Predicate

Chapter 3   Sentence Building

Name_____ Date _____

Fixing Fragments

Read the book *Mufaro's Beautiful Daughters* by John Steptoe. Use sentence parts taken from the tale to write new, complete sentences. (Sentences do not have to match the sentences in the book.)

"The Beginning" and "The Messenger"

Subject (fragment)	Add a predicate.
A man named Mufaro	
Manyara	
Nyasha	
One day a messenger	
The king	
Mufaro	

Part B

"Manyara's Journey" and "Nyasha's Journey"

Add a subject.	Predicate (fragment)
	give me something to eat.
	have only enough for myself.
	looked at the trees and laughed out loud.
	must be hungry.
	gave her a small pouch with seeds.
	bravely made her way to the chamber.

Chapter 3 Sentence Building

Name_____ Date_____

Simple Sentences

A simple sentence has a subject (naming part) on one side and the predicate (telling part) on the other side. Two samples have been done for you. Write four more sentences to share with the class.

Jade	wrote a story about a giraffe.
subject	predicate

Julian	worked with magnets at the science center.
subject	predicate

subject	predicate

subject	predicate

subject	predicate

subject	predicate

©Teacher Created Resources, Inc.

Chapter 3   Sentence Building

Name_____   Date_____

Simple Sentences with Two Subjects

A simple sentence can have two subjects (naming parts) on one side with the predicate (telling part) on the other side. Two samples have been done for you. Write four more sentences to share with the class.

Malika and Susan	wrote word lists for the story.
subjects	predicate

Famah and Alex	found information about frogs.
subjects	predicate

subjects	predicate

subjects	predicate

subjects	predicate

subjects	predicate

Chapter 3   Sentence Building

Name_____   Date_____

Simple Sentences with Two Subjects and Two Predicates

A simple sentence can have two subjects (naming parts) on one side and two predicates (telling parts) on the other side. Two samples have been done for you. Write four more sentences to share with the class.

Su Lin and Jorge	created a mural and hung it in the hall.
subjects	predicates

Jose and Jamie	ate lunch and cleaned up the kitchen.
subjects	predicates

subjects	predicates

subjects	predicates

subjects	predicates

subjects	predicates

©Teacher Created Resources, Inc.   #3543 Classroom Authoring Guided Writing

Chapter 3   Sentence Building

Name_____   Date_____

Compound Sentences Using Conjunctions–*and, but, or*

A compound sentence has a simple sentence with a subject and predicate on one side and a simple sentence with another subject and predicate on the other side. The two sentences can be joined together with a comma and a conjunction in the middle. Three samples have been done for you. Write three more compound sentences to share with the class.

Farerra did an experiment,	and	May wrote a report.
simple sentence	conjunction	simple sentence

Nina can run well,	but	she does not like to jump rope.
simple sentence	conjunction	simple sentence

Luis could read a poetry book,	or	he could write a poem.
simple sentence	conjunction	simple sentence

_____	_____	_____
simple sentence	conjunction	simple sentence

_____	_____	_____
simple sentence	conjunction	simple sentence

_____	_____	_____
simple sentence	conjunction	simple sentence

Chapter 3 Sentence Building

Name_____ Date_____

Statement Sentences

A Cool Pet

Statement sentences are telling sentences. They tell the reader something. Write a statement sentence for each number. Use a capital letter at the beginning and a period at the end. A sample answer for the first number has been done for you.

Max is a cool pet horse because he does tricks.

1. Write a statement sentence that tells about a wonderful pet.

   _____
   _____
   _____

2. Write a statement sentence that tells what supplies you will need for this pet.

   _____
   _____
   _____

3. Write a statement sentence that tells how to take care of this pet.

   _____
   _____
   _____

4. Write a statement sentence that tells how a person can get one of these pets.

   _____
   _____
   _____

Chapter 3   *Sentence Building*

Name_____   Date_____

Question Sentences

A Cool Pet

In question sentences, the reader or listener must give an answer. Write a question sentence for each number. Use a capital letter at the beginning and a question mark at the end. A sample sentence for the first number has been done for you.

How do you give a horse a bath?

1. Write a question sentence that asks someone for instructions about this pet's care.

   _____
   _____
   _____

2. Write a question sentence that asks if a shopping center has supplies for this pet's care.

   _____
   _____
   _____

3. Write a question sentence that asks the name of the pet store.

   _____
   _____
   _____

4. Write a question sentence that asks if the pet store gives classes in pet care.

   _____
   _____
   _____

Chapter 3　　　　　　　　　　　　　　　　　　　　　Sentence Building

Name_____　　　Date_____

Command Sentences

A Cool Pet

In command sentences, the writer is giving an order, or command. Remember to be polite when writing command sentences. Write a command sentence for each number. Use a capital letter at the beginning and a period at the end. A sample answer for the first number has been done for you.

You must buy a curry brush to groom a horse's coat.

1. Write a command sentence that tells which supplies to buy to clean your pet.

   _____
   _____
   _____

2. Write a command sentence that tells what to do first.

   _____
   _____
   _____

3. Write a command sentence that tells what to do next.

   _____
   _____
   _____

4. Write a command sentence that tells what to do last.

   _____
   _____
   _____

©Teacher Created Resources, Inc.　　　　　　　　　　#3543 Classroom Authoring Guided Writing

Chapter 3   Sentence Building

Name_____   Date_____

Exclamation Sentences

A Cool Pet

Exclamation sentences show strong feeling. Write an exclamation sentence for each number. Use a capital letter at the beginning and an exclamation mark at the end. A sample answer for the first number has been done for you.

Be careful while riding the horse or it might throw you off!

1. Write an exclamation sentence that tells someone about a danger related to your pet.

   _____
   _____
   _____

2. Write an exclamation sentence that tells someone to be careful while handling the pet.

   _____
   _____
   _____

3. Write an exclamation sentence that tells someone about something they should never do to the pet.

   _____
   _____
   _____

4. Write an exclamation sentence that tells someone they did a great job with the pet.

   _____
   _____
   _____

Writing Paragraphs

A paragraph is a group of related sentences that come together to form a thought. The paragraph is the basic building block of stories, reports, and essays. A paragraph that stands alone has a beginning, middle, and ending. Paragraphs linked together in a report or story often use the beginnings and endings of individual paragraphs as transitions.

If You Want It, Model It!

Graphic organizers are good planning devices for young writers who are still functioning in the concrete stage. However, the students also need to see paragraph writing repeatedly modeled by the teacher. Modeling paragraph writing is probably the single most important thing a teacher can do to help both the proficient and the emerging writer.

When teaching paragraph writing, the teacher also needs to help the students begin with the end in mind, sometimes referred to as backward design or whole-to-part. The writers decide what the end product will be (e.g., paragraph, story), what it will look like, its length, the audience, and the overall tone of the product. These decisions guide the selection of a graphic organizer and the collection of ideas.

The 6 Questions

The 6 Questions: Who, What, When, Where, Why, and How allow the students to find answers to the provided prompts and help develop questioning as a strategy for gathering information (pages 44–51).

COW Strategy

The COW strategy helps the students collect, organize, and write paragraphs (pages 54–63). See pages 52–53 for detailed directions on modeling this strategy.

Draw, Collect, Organize & Write Strategy

For this strategy, the students will use the COW Strategy and add drawing to it. The students will draw about their topic, collect ideas, organize them, and then write (see pages 64–67).

Writing Assessment

Remember—writing is a process. Quality products require the students to work through the writing process to develop that product. The teacher should not grade every dimension of writing for every assignment.

> **Note:** If possible, make 11" x 17" copies of the paragraph-writing lessons for each student (e.g., pages 56–57). Young children benefit from seeing the strategy and the entire writing process worked out in front of them. Large paper allows them to see the big picture of the writing process and how the writing stages work together. It also allows for the size of the students' handwriting. (If 11" x 17" paper is not available, copy the lessons onto separate sheets so the students can have the two sheets side by side.)

Chapter 4　　　　　　　　　　　　　　　　　　　　　　　　　　　　　　　　Writing Paragraphs

Name_____　　　Date_____

Fairy Tale

6 Questions

Write about a favorite fairy tale or story you have read. The "W" prompts will guide you in writing sentences. Remember to write complete sentences and use capitals and end marks. Each sentence must have a "naming part" (subject) and a "telling part" (predicate).

Who	
What	
When	
Where	
Why	
How	

　　A. **Pop** words or ideas in, out, or around.

　　B. Hold a peer or teacher conference to **polish** your writing.

　　C. Finally, write a neat draft on page 45 to **publish** your work.

#3543 Classroom Authoring Guided Writing　　　　　　　　　　　　©Teacher Created Resources, Inc.

Chapter 4   *Writing Paragraphs*

Name _____ **Date** _____

Fairy Tale (cont.)

→ *My favorite fairy tale or story is* _____

Chapter 4   Writing Paragraphs

Name_____   Date _____

My Sick Friend

6 Questions

Your friend is sick and you would like to do something special for him or her. The "W" prompts will guide you in writing sentences. Use the prompts to plan a special surprise for your friend. Remember to write complete sentences and use capitals and end marks. Each sentence must have a "naming part" (subject) and a "telling part" (predicate).

Who	
What	
When	
Where	
Why	
How	

A. **Pop** words or ideas in, out, or around.

B. Hold a peer or teacher conference to **polish** your writing.

C. Finally, write a neat draft on page 47 to **publish** your work.

My Sick Friend (cont.)

→ *I just learned that my friend has been sick.*

Chapter 4   *Writing Paragraphs*

Name_____   Date_____

The Wishing Star

6 Questions

Imagine you looked up in the sky late one evening and saw the first star in the sky. You think of the poem, *Star light, star bright/ The first star I see tonight/ I wish I may, I wish I might/ Have the wish I wish tonight.* What would you wish for? The "W" prompts will guide you in writing sentences. Use your imagination. Remember to write complete sentences and use capitals and end marks. Each sentence must have a "naming part" (subject) and a "telling part" (predicate).

Who	
What	
When	
Where	
Why	
How	

A. **Pop** words or ideas in, out, or around.
B. Hold a peer or teacher conference to **polish** your writing.
C. Finally, write a neat draft on page 49 to **publish** your work.

Name _____ Date _____

The Wishing Star (cont.)

→ *When I saw the first star in the sky,*
I made a wish that _____

_____

_____

_____

_____

_____

_____

_____

Star light, star bright,

The first star I see tonight,

I wish I may, I wish I might,

Have the wish I wish tonight.

Chapter 4   Writing Paragraphs

Name _____   Date _____

_____
Topic

Blank 6 Questions Form

Choose your own topic or a topic the teacher assigns. Explore the topic by answering the "W" questions in the boxes below. Remember to write complete sentences and use capitals and end marks. Each sentence must have a "naming part" (subject) and a "telling part" (predicate).

Who	
What	
When	
Where	
Why	
How	

A. **Pop** words or ideas in, out, or around.

B. Hold a peer or teacher conference to **polish** your writing.

C. Finally, write a neat draft on page 51 to **publish** your work.

D. Draw a picture in the box about the paragraph.

Chapter 4 *Writing Paragraphs*

Name _____   **Date** _____

Topic

COW Strategy

The acronym COW stands for **C**ollect, **O**rganize, and **W**rite. Just as the students need practice in reading and math, they must also have many experiences writing sentences, paragraphs, and stories before they master the craft of writing. When the students practice writing paragraphs using the COW strategy, they learn and practice writing as a process: collecting ideas, organizing the ideas, and finally writing sentences about the ideas.

Guided Writing Using the COW Strategy

The teacher guides sentence development and models it (using transparency film, a fine-point marker, and an overhead projector) while the students write along. As a student progresses, the teacher will give more freedom to the student to write his or her own sentences.

Directions for the Teacher

1. **Collection Steps**

   A. Discuss the topic. Write the topic in the center circle of the web.

   B. Prompt the students to generate ideas that go with the topic. Write these ideas beside the web.

   C. Guide the class in deciding on the ideas that fit with the main idea of the topic. Write them on the spokes around the center circle of the web.

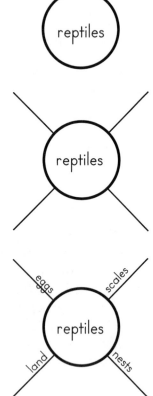

2. **Organizing Steps**

   A. Have the students help decide on the order for the ideas. Number the ideas on the web.

   B. Make a separate list of the ideas.

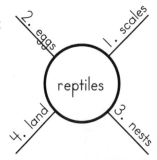

Chapter 4 — Writing Paragraphs

COW Strategy (cont.)

Guided Writing Using the COW Strategy (cont.)

Directions for the Teacher (cont.)

3. Writing Steps

   A. Always write a topic sentence (from the center circle of the web) first.

   B. Write a sentence about item one, item two, item three, and so on, until finished.

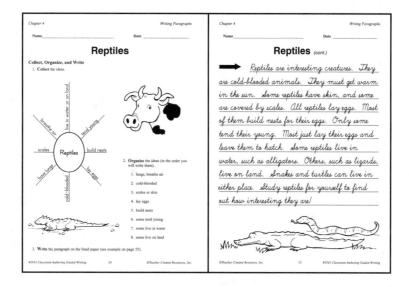

Note: If possible, make 11" x 17" copies of the COW paragraph-writing lessons for each student. Young children benefit from seeing the strategy and the entire writing process worked out in front of them. Large paper allows them to see the big picture of the writing process and how the writing stages work together. It also allows for the size of the students' handwriting. (If 11" x 17" paper is not available, copy the lessons onto separate sheets so the students can have the two sheets side by side.)

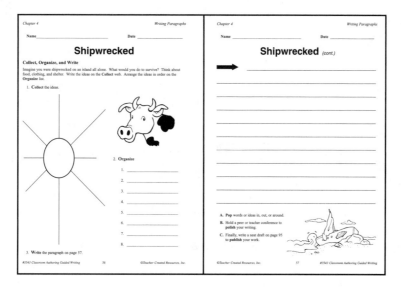

Chapter 4   Writing Paragraphs

Name_____   Date_____

Reptiles

Collect, Organize, and Write

1. **Collect** the ideas.

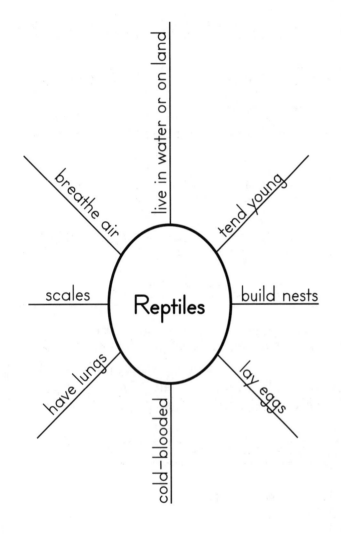

2. **Organize** the ideas (in the order you will write them).

   1. cold-blooded
   2. scales or skin
   3. lay eggs
   4. build nests
   5. some tend young
   6. some live in water
   7. some live on land
   8. some live on land and in water

3. **Write** the paragraph on the lined paper (see example on page 55).

#3543 Classroom Authoring Guided Writing   54   ©Teacher Created Resources, Inc.

Chapter 4   Writing Paragraphs

Name_____   Date_____

Reptiles (cont.)

➡ Reptiles are interesting creatures. They are cold-blooded animals. They must get warm in the sun. Some reptiles have skin, and some are covered by scales. All reptiles lay eggs. Most of them build nests for their eggs. Only some tend their young. Most just lay their eggs and leave them to hatch. Some reptiles live in water, such as alligators. Others, such as lizards, live on land. Snakes and turtles can live in either place. Study reptiles for yourself to find out how interesting they are!

Chapter 4   *Writing Paragraphs*

Name _____ Date _____

Shipwrecked

Collect, Organize, and Write

Imagine you were shipwrecked on an island all alone. What would you do to survive? Think about food, clothing, and shelter. Write the ideas on the **Collect** web. Arrange the ideas in order on the **Organize** list.

1. **Collect** the ideas.

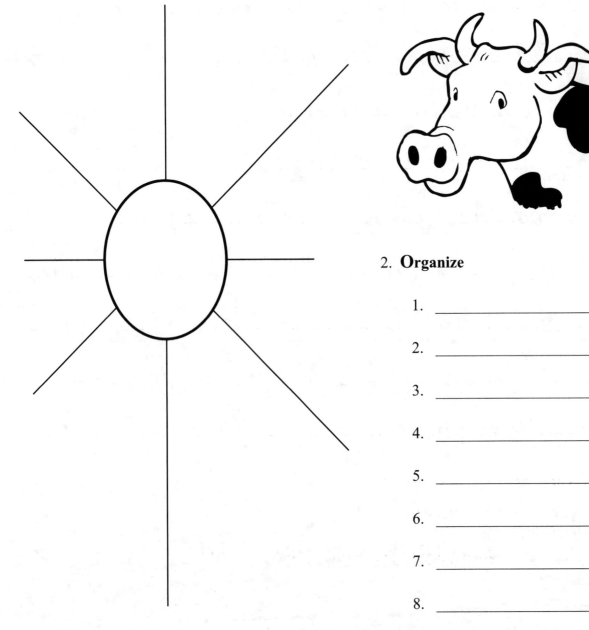

2. **Organize**

   1. _____
   2. _____
   3. _____
   4. _____
   5. _____
   6. _____
   7. _____
   8. _____

3. **Write** the paragraph on page 57.

Chapter 4 Writing Paragraphs

Name _____ Date _____

Shipwrecked (cont.)

➡ _____
_____
_____
_____
_____
_____
_____
_____
_____
_____
_____
_____

A. **Pop** words or ideas in, out, or around.

B. Hold a peer or teacher conference to **polish** your writing.

C. Finally, write a neat draft to **publish** your work.

©Teacher Created Resources, Inc. #3543 Classroom Authoring Guided Writing

Chapter 4 Writing Paragraphs

Name _____ Date _____

My Garden

Collect, Organize, and Write

Think about a garden you could create. It might be a flower garden, vegetable garden, rock garden, butterfly garden, or memory garden. Write about what you could put in the garden, how you would care for it, what it could be used for, and how you would share it. Write the ideas on the **Collect** web. Arrange the ideas in order on the **Organize** list.

1. **Collect** the ideas.

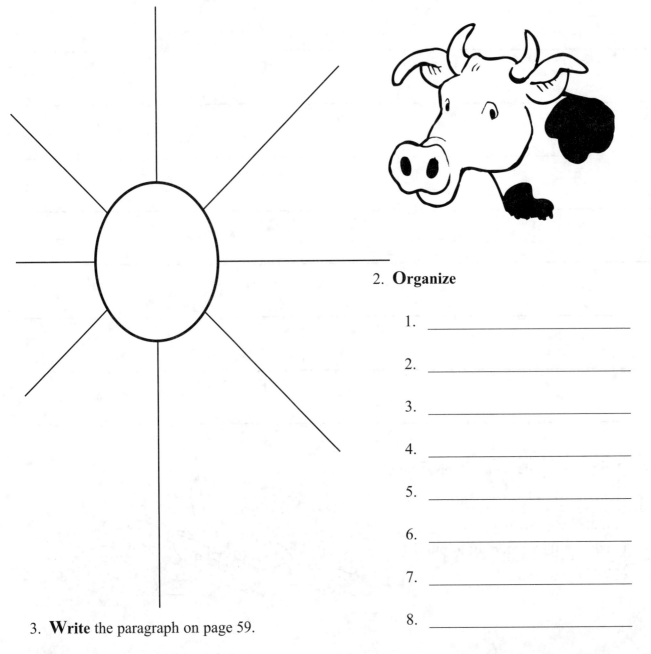

2. **Organize**

   1. _____
   2. _____
   3. _____
   4. _____
   5. _____
   6. _____
   7. _____
   8. _____

3. **Write** the paragraph on page 59.

#3543 Classroom Authoring Guided Writing   58   ©Teacher Created Resources, Inc.

Chapter 4　　　　　　　　　　　　　　　　　　　　　　　　　　　　　　　*Writing Paragraphs*

Name _____　　　　　**Date** _____

My Garden (cont.)

➡ _____

_____

_____

_____

_____

_____

_____

_____

_____

_____

_____

A. **Pop** words or ideas in, out, or around.

B. Hold a peer or teacher conference to **polish** your writing.

C. Finally, write a neat draft to **publish** your work.

©Teacher Created Resources, Inc.　　　　59　　　　#3543 *Classroom Authoring Guided Writing*

Chapter 4   Writing Paragraphs

Name_____   Date _____

Monster Sandwich

Collect, Organize, and Write

A monster sandwich has lots of ingredients and takes different utensils to make it. How would you make the sandwich, what would you put on it, and how would you serve it? Who would help you eat it? Write the ideas on the **Collect** web. Arrange the ideas in order on the **Organize** list.

1. **Collect** the ideas.

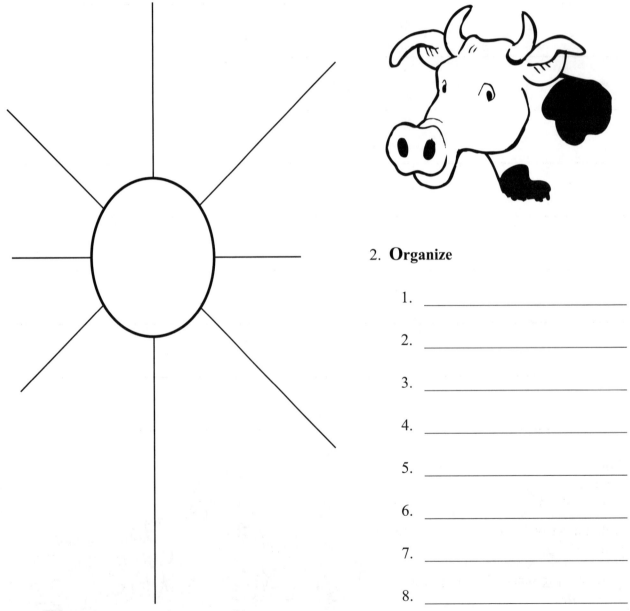

2. **Organize**

    1. _____
    2. _____
    3. _____
    4. _____
    5. _____
    6. _____
    7. _____
    8. _____

3. **Write** the paragraph on page 61.

#3543 Classroom Authoring Guided Writing   60   ©Teacher Created Resources, Inc.

Chapter 4 Writing Paragraphs

Name _____   Date _____

Monster Sandwich (cont.)

➡ _____
_____
_____
_____
_____
_____
_____
_____
_____
_____
_____
_____

A. **Pop** words or ideas in, out, or around.

B. Hold a peer or teacher conference to **polish** your writing.

C. Finally, write a neat draft to **publish** your work.

Chapter 4 Writing Paragraphs

Name _____ Date _____

_____
Topic

Blank COW Strategy Form

1. **Collect** the ideas.

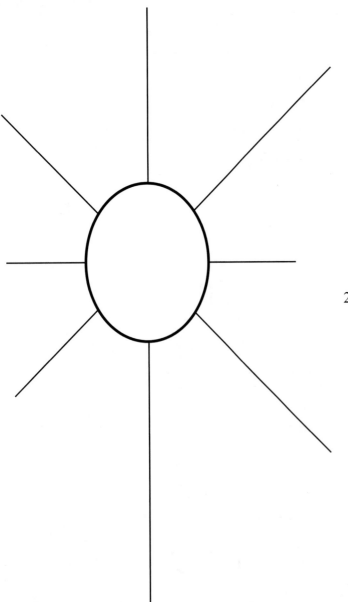

2. **Organize** the ideas (in the order you will write them).

1. _____
2. _____
3. _____
4. _____
5. _____
6. _____
7. _____
8. _____

3. **Write** the paragraph on page 63.
4. **Draw** a picture about your paragraph in the box.

Chapter 4 *Writing Paragraphs*

Name _____ **Date** _____

_____
Topic

→ _____

_____

_____

_____

_____

_____

_____

_____

_____

_____

Chapter 4 · Writing Paragraphs

Name _____   Date _____

My Room

Draw, Collect, Organize, and Write

Use what you know about the COW Strategy, and now add drawing to it. Close your eyes and imagine your room, where the doors and windows are and where the furnishings and other items are. Next, draw your room in the box. Write ideas about your room on the **Collect** web. Arrange the ideas in order on the **Organize** list.

A. Draw

B. Collect

C. Organize

1. _____
2. _____
3. _____
4. _____
5. _____
6. _____
7. _____
8. _____

B. Write your draft on page 65.

#3543 Classroom Authoring Guided Writing　　64　　©Teacher Created Resources, Inc.

Chapter 4　　　　　　　　　　　　　　　　　　　　　　　　　　Writing Paragraphs

Name _____　　**Date** _____

My Room (cont.)

➡ _____

_____

_____

_____

_____

_____

_____

_____

_____

_____

_____

A. **Pop** words or ideas in, out, or around.

B. Hold a peer or teacher conference to **polish** your writing.

C. Finally, write a neat draft to **publish** your work.

Chapter 4   *Writing Paragraphs*

Name _____   Date _____

                     _____
                                    Title

Draw, Collect, Organize, and Write

Use what you know about the COW Strategy, and now add drawing to it. Using a topic of your own or from the teacher, draw about your idea in the box. Write ideas about your room on the **Collect** web. Arrange the ideas in order on the **Organize** list.

A. Draw

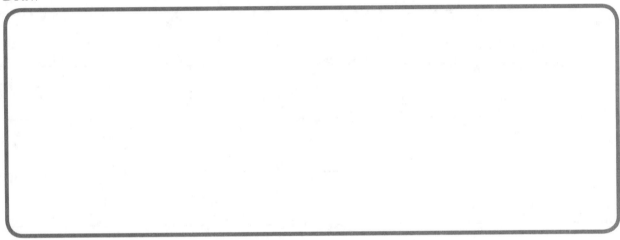

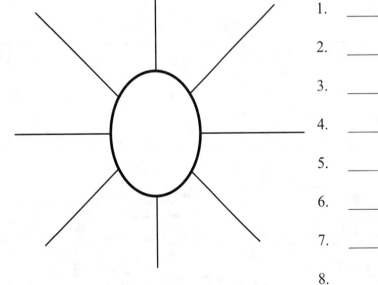

C. Organize

1. _____
2. _____
3. _____
4. _____
5. _____
6. _____
7. _____
8. _____

D. Write your draft on page 67. Draw a picture about your paragraph in the box.

Beginning   **Middle**   **Ending**

#3543 *Classroom Authoring Guided Writing*   ©*Teacher Created Resources, Inc.*

Chapter 4 | Writing Paragraphs

Name _____   Date _____

_____
Title

→ _____

_____

_____

_____

_____

_____

_____

_____

A. **Pop** words or ideas in, out, or around.

B. Hold a peer or teacher conference to **polish** your writing.

C. Finally, write a neat draft to **publish** your work.

Chapter 5   *Journaling*

Introduction to Journaling

Regular journaling is an effective way to integrate writing across the curriculum. A student owns his or her journal and takes pride in its contents. Journaling may also include student drawings and graphic organizers. The journaling activities in this chapter (see pages 69–74) will keep the students' writing skills sharp and emphasize that writing should be part of everyday life.

Daily Journaling

Make multiple copies of Daily Journaling (page 69) for each student to keep in his or her binder. The teacher may have the students write on this form at the beginning of class for several minutes each day. Randomly select three students to share their responses each day to ensure that the students participate. Respect any student who does not wish to read his or her journal. Once a week, ask the students to hand in their journals. Take time to scan them. Daily journaling is similar to diary writing; a student who wants a selection to be private can fold the page lengthwise.

Character Journaling

As in other types of journaling, character journaling helps the students develop higher-order thinking. The students learn to think like the characters and act like the author. On the Character Journaling sheet (page 70), the students pose questions for the characters in a story and imagine what the characters' responses will be. Then the students imagine the characters asking them questions and write their own responses. This is a fun way to help the students gain a better understanding of character development.

Student-Teacher and Student-Parent Journaling

Use the Student-Teacher Journaling sheet (page 71) to have an ongoing dialog about any topic. With this activity, the teacher can assess a student's knowledge of a concept and writing ability. This gives the teacher a chance to get to know the student and his or her strengths, abilities, and interests. It is also an opportunity for the teacher to provide individualized motivation for the student. In the same manner, a parent can communicate with his or her child using the Student-Parent Journaling sheet (page 72). This could be a place to discuss homework, a reflection of what is happening at school, or a special place where parent and child leave each other messages.

My Friend and I Journaling

The My Friend and I Journaling sheet (page 73) provides a good opportunity for two students to journal with each other. It is a good alternative to note-passing. The teacher may need to set guidelines and make sure each student participates.

Respond to Action

The students can use the Respond to Action sheet (page 74) to journal after an argument or disagreement. It can also serve as a follow-up for social studies lessons, or community, national, or world events.

Other Ways to Use Journaling

• Analyze data	• Explore imagination	• Provide feedback for other students
• Assist comprehension	• Interact with peers	• Respond to events
• Collect information	• Listing story ideas	• Self-reflect
• Debate	• Log a project	• Solve problems
• Evaluate literature	• Ongoing dialog with tutor	• Think deeply

Name _____

Daily Journaling

Date _____

_____
_____
_____
_____
_____
_____
_____

Date _____

_____
_____
_____
_____
_____
_____
_____

Date _____

_____
_____
_____
_____
_____
_____
_____

Chapter 5   *Journaling*

Name _____   Date _____

Character Journaling

Characters in a story have reasons for their actions. Pretend you talked to the characters. Write three questions you would ask one of the characters. Then write how you think that character would answer. Next, write three questions that character might ask you and how you would respond to each question.

	Your Question	Character's Answer
1.		
2.		
3.		
	Character's Question	**Your Answer**
1.		
2.		
3.		

Student-Teacher Journaling

Name _____

Date _____

Date	Student	Teacher

Student-Parent Journaling

Name _____ Date _____

Date	Student	Parent

Chapter 5 — Journaling

Name _____ Date _____

My Friend and I Journaling

Date	My Friend: _____										
	Me: _____										

Chapter 5   Journaling

Name _____ Date _____

Respond to Action

Action What happened?	My First Response before thinking	My Final Judgment after careful thought

Writing Essays and Reports

In Chapter 4 (Writing Paragraphs), the teacher gradually took less responsibility while the student assumed more responsibility for a writing assignment. At the end of the chapter, the students wrote paragraphs with less and less guidance from the teacher. This chapter is devoted to guiding the students through writing essays and reports. When the students write two and three related paragraphs, they are really writing essays, reports, and in the next chapter, stories.

Like paragraphs, essays and reports need a beginning, middle, and ending. Different paragraphs can come together under a main idea to form essays and reports. They flow together using transitional devices that lead the reader from one thought to the next.

Modeled Writing

Guided writing makes good use of the writing process; it allows the teacher to lead the students through the writing process while demonstrating and modeling the lesson. The first lessons should be modeled—whole class lessons with the teacher modeling and the class contributing and writing along. The students then practice what they have seen under the guidance of the teacher.

Guided writing is controlled writing—the very best of scaffolding. In modeling essay writing, the teacher keeps tight control of every sentence in the project and does not allow the students to work ahead or fall behind. Although the teacher may be allowing the students to write individual responses to sentence prompts, he or she may demonstrate and model the type of sentence that comes next and ask for verbal examples to ensure that the students have an understanding of what they are to do before they start to write.

Once all the students are ready to write, you may use a timed writing technique. After discussion and instruction about a particular sentence, the teacher can say, "You have 90 seconds to write this sentence once I say 'go.' When time is up, I will ask if you need 15 more seconds. If you are not finished and need more time, do not talk; raise your hand, and get back to work. All others will remain quiet until I call time. Remember capitals and end marks. Ready . . . begin." The teacher may ask who needs more time again if needed.

When using guided writing for essays, do not assign the whole essay. Instead, model only one stage at a time, following the format provided in this chapter. (See a sample writing lesson on pages 76–79.) Keep the students on the same sentence inside the essay. Give directions, provide class samples and models, and allow the students enough time to complete that sentence. With each lesson in essay writing, gradually release responsibility to the students for particular parts.

Essay Writing Lessons

A graphic organizer is provided on the first page of each essay lesson in this chapter. (See pages 80–89.) For this chapter, the organizers are picture webs. This visual aspect makes collecting ideas more concrete to the young writer. Essays and reports have a distinct beginning, middle, and ending. For each of these lessons, discuss the beginning and how it introduces the main idea. Also discuss the ending and how it summarizes or provides closure to the main idea.

Beginnings and endings have been provided for the students. Feel free to improve upon them or revise them; however, the focus of this chapter on essay writing for beginners is on collecting ideas and writing the middle part.

Chapter 6 — Essays and Reports

Sample Essay Writing Lesson

Winter Fun

1. **Indoors**
   - read books
   - do crafts
   - bake cookies
   - sit by fire
2. **Outdoors**
   - sledding
   - snow fort
   - ice skate
   - ski
3. **At School**
   - art
   - basketball
   - drama
   - dance teams

Directions (for the teacher)

1. Discuss the main idea of fun winter activities.
2. Solicit ideas from the students (see picture web on page 77).
3. Number the ideas for the middle by section (e.g., 1—Indoors, 2—Outdoors, 3—At School).
4. Guide the students, sentence by sentence, to write each sentence on the corresponding essay page.
5. Use timed writing (see Modeled Writing on page 75).
6. Get student feedback by having them read their sentences as you progress through the essay.
7. Writing an essay may take several sessions. When you return to the essay, make sure to read what you wrote previously and find your place on the picture web.

Chapter 6 — Essays and Reports

Name _____ Date _____

Sample Essay Writing Lesson (cont.)

Winter Fun (cont.)

Beginning
→ Winter is a special time of year. Winter means cold weather, snow, and ice, but it can also mean exciting activities indoors and outdoors.

Middle
→ We spend more time indoors in winter. Indoor winter activities can be fun.

Chapter 6 — Essays and Reports

Name _____ Date _____

Sample Essay Writing Lesson (cont.)

Winter Fun (cont.)

Middle (cont.)
Outdoor winter activities are fun also. Winter can be fun at school. If you are not allowed outside you can play games.

Ending
Do not dread winter. Instead, enjoy the fun activities that you can do during winter.

A. **Pop** words or ideas in, out, or around.
B. Hold a peer or teacher conference to **polish** your writing.
C. Finally, write a clean draft to **publish** your work.

Chapter 6   *Essays and Reports*

Name _____   **Date** _____

Sample Essay Writing Lesson (cont.)

Winter Fun (cont.)

By the snowman's head, list four things you can do inside in winter.

By the snowman's middle, list four things you can do outside in winter.

By the snowman's bottom, list four things you can do at school in winter.

Chapter 6   *Essays and Reports*

Name _____   Date _____

Sample Essay Writing Lesson (cont.)

Winter Fun (cont.)

Beginning

Winter is a special time of year. Winter means cold weather, snow, and ice, but it can also mean exciting activities indoors and outdoors.

Middle

We spend more time indoors in winter. Indoor winter activities can be fun.

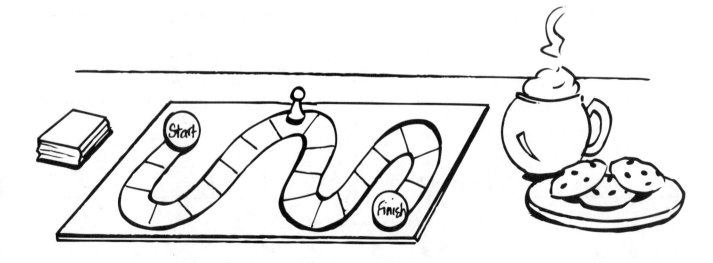

#3543 Classroom Authoring Guided Writing   78   ©Teacher Created Resources, Inc.

Chapter 6 — Essays and Reports

Name _____ Date _____

Sample Essay Writing Lesson (cont.)

Winter Fun (cont.)

Middle (cont.)

Outdoor winter activities are fun also. Winter can be fun at school. If you are not allowed outside you can play games.

Ending

Do not dread winter. Instead, enjoy the fun activities that you can do during winter.

A. **Pop** words or ideas in, out, or around.

B. Hold a peer or teacher conference to **polish** your writing.

C. Finally, write a clean draft to **publish** your work.

Chapter 6   Essays and Reports

Name _____   Date _____

Spring

The weather warms up in spring and people go outdoors more. There are many fun activities to look forward to in spring. Collect two ideas for each topic on each of the five flower petals. Then write about spring on page 81.

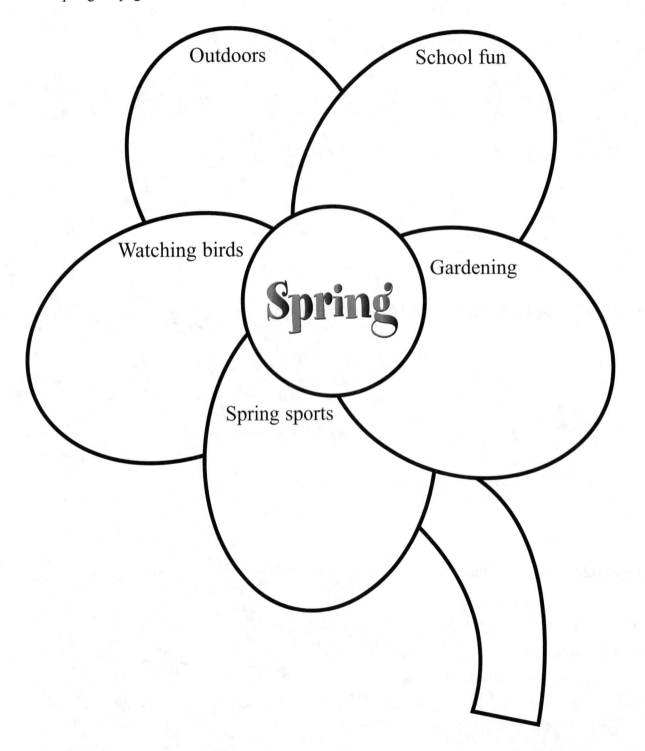

Chapter 6 — Essays and Reports

Name _____   Date _____

Spring *(cont.)*

→ The weather warms up in the spring and people go outdoors more. There are many fun activities to look forward to in spring.

I can't wait to go outdoors when the weather warms up. Just being outside is

At school, when the weather warms up we get to

I enjoy getting outdoors to look at the flowers and trees.

Birds migrate to my neighborhood to build their nests and raise their babies.

Last, I get to go outdoors to play sports.

Perhaps spring is my favorite season. I enjoy the weather warming up and the opportunity to do spring activities once again.

A. **Pop** words or ideas in, out, or around.
B. Hold a peer or teacher conference to **polish** your writing.
C. Finally, write a neat draft to **publish** your work.

Chapter 6   *Essays and Reports*

Name _____   **Date** _____

Star Teacher

You have the chance to design a super teacher! On the lines of the star, write traits that you would like in a Star Teacher. Then, put numbers beside each trait in the order you plan to write about the Star Teacher. Some samples have been provided. Finally, write about your Star Teacher on page 83.

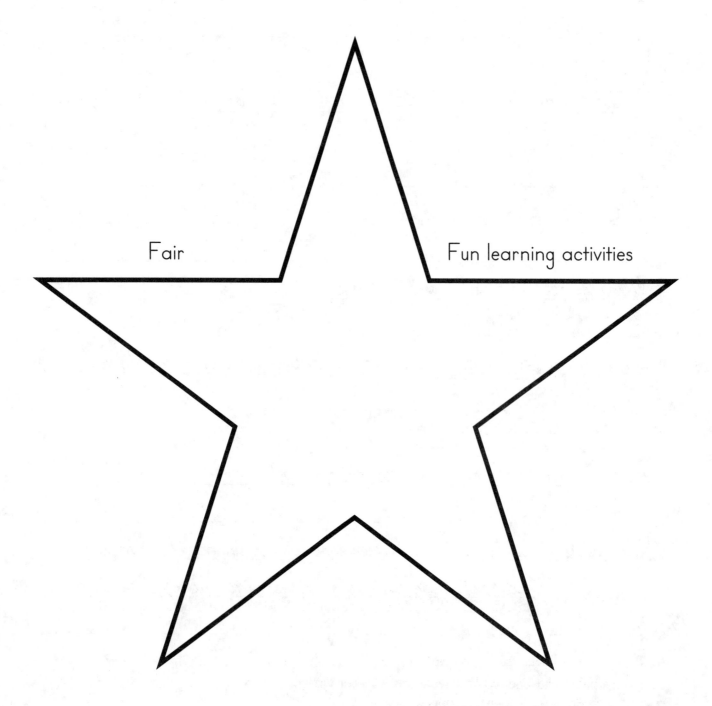

Chapter 6 *Essays and Reports*

Name _____   Date _____

Star Teacher (cont.)

→ Teachers are important to a child. My teacher is a star teacher. There are at least five good reasons that learning is enjoyable and fun with my teacher.

First,

Next,

Also,

After that,

Finally,

Do you agree that my teacher is a star?

A. Pop words or ideas in, out, or around.
B. Hold a peer or teacher conference to **polish** your writing.
C. Finally, write a neat draft to **publish** your work.

Chapter 6 *Essays and Reports*

Name _____ **Date** _____

Family Photo

Draw a picture of three family members in the picture frame below. Write their names and three things that are special about each person on the picture. Write about your family photo on page 85.

Chapter 6 Essays and Reports

Name _____ Date _____

Family Photo (cont.)

→ *Families are special. Each member is important. Take a look at my family portrait.*

First,

Next,

Last,

Draw your own family portrait and think about why each member is important. It may surprise you!

- A. **Pop** words or ideas in, out, or around.
- B. Hold a peer or teacher conference to **polish** your writing.
- C. Finally, write a neat draft to **publish** your work.

©Teacher Created Resources, Inc.   #3543 Classroom Authoring Guided Writing

Chapter 6　　　　　　　　　　　　　　　　　　　　　　　　　　　Essays and Reports

Name _____　　Date _____

Fitness and Fun

Three popular sports can help keep you fit and healthy. They are also a lot of fun! Write details about each sport below. Then write about these fitness activities on page 87.

Running and Track

_____
_____
_____
_____
_____

Soccer

_____
_____
_____
_____
_____

Basketball

_____
_____
_____
_____

#3543 Classroom Authoring Guided Writing　　　　　©Teacher Created Resources, Inc.

Chapter 6 · Essays and Reports

Name _____ **Date** _____

Fitness and Fun (cont.)

→ *Three popular sports can help keep you fit and healthy. They are also fun. Track, soccer, and basketball can be played by girls, boys, men, or women.*

First, track

Next, soccer

Last, basketball

Try one or all of these sports to keep physically fit. Have fun learning these sports, and spending time with friends.

A. **Pop** words or ideas in, out, or around.
B. Hold a peer or teacher conference to **polish** your writing.
C. Finally, write a neat draft to **publish** your work.

©Teacher Created Resources, Inc. · #3543 *Classroom Authoring Guided Writing*

Chapter 6 Essays and Reports

Name _____ Date _____

Transportation

Transportation is important to the country. Trucks, ships, and planes carry things that people need. List items each vehicle transports. Then write about these forms of transportation on page 89.

Trucks carry:

_____

_____

_____

_____

Ships carry:

_____

_____

_____

_____

Planes carry:

_____

_____

_____

_____

Chapter 6   *Essays and Reports*

Name _____   **Date** _____

Transportation (cont.)

➡️ Transportation is important to my country. Trucks, ships, and planes carry people and things that we need to live and work.

Trucks

Ships

Planes

The next time you meet a truck driver, ship captain, or airplane pilot, be sure to thank him or her!

- **A. Pop** words or ideas in, out, or around.
- **B.** Hold a peer or teacher conference to **polish** your writing.
- **C.** Finally, write a neat draft to **publish** your work.

Chapter 7   Story Writing

Story Writing

Using Story Planners

An excellent way to introduce the story writing process is to retell a familiar story using a story planner. The students do not have to simultaneously attend to creating a new story while becoming familiar with story elements (e.g., characters, setting) and story sections (e.g., beginning, ending). They simply identify those elements and sections in a familiar story and write the ideas on a story planner. For practice retelling stories, have the students complete the Story Planner sheet on page 93.

After the students have used story planners to retell stories, they can begin to create elements for an original story using the same strategies. A list of story writing ideas is provided on page 96. Write several class stories with the students before withdrawing support. (See an example of a class-guided written story on this page and pages 91–92.) Give each student a copy of the Story Planner sheets (pages 93–94) to plan his or her own story. Have the students write their final drafts on a copy of page 95.

Class Guided Writing: Austin's Bicycle

Step 1: Plan

A. As a class, fill out a STAR Vocabulary chart for the story (see example below). You may have the students make their own charts using the directions on page 23, or provide a copy of page 24 for each student.

Sensory Words	Technical Words	Active Words	Real Talk
friends riding greasy grass smell	wheelie ramp donut helmet	jump race speed ride	"You may borrow my bike." "I brought you some bike parts."

B. Give each student a copy of page 93 to complete as you plan each element for the class-guided story writing.

  1. **Problem**—Develop a problem with a realistic ending.
     A boy wants his own bicycle.
  2. **Solution**—Determine a possible solution to the problem.
     The boy does odd jobs to earn money to buy a bicycle.
  3. and 4. **Characters and Setting**—Develop or use previously developed characters and setting.
     Austin, Isabel, Julio; Austin's neighborhood, current day
  5. **Middle Adventures**—Plan the middle section by creating attempts to solve the problem.
     a. Austin asks his parents for a bicycle, but they say no.
     b. Austin borrows his cousin's bike, but his cousin wants it back.
     c. Austin finds some bike parts to build a bicycle.
  6. **Epilog**—Plan what happens after the problem is solved.
     From then on, when Austin wants something, he knows he can work hard to earn the money for it.

Chapter 7   Story Writing

Story Writing (cont.)

Class Guided Writing: Austin's Bicycle (cont.)

Step 2: Package

Instruct the students to write the story from the beginning to the ending. The story beginning should include the characters, setting, and problem. The story middle includes a series of adventures where the characters are trying to solve the problem. The students should then write the story ending, following the plan they have previously made for a solution.

Beginning

Austin sat alone beside the tree watching the kids ride their bikes. One friend was riding his red bike on the sidewalk. Another friend could do wheelies and spin around. All the kids in the neighborhood could do donuts. Isabel was riding her silver bike. She could jump the ramp and land a bunny hop. Austin really wanted his own bicycle.

Middle

Adventure #1

On Saturday, Austin had breakfast with his family.

"Mom, Dad, I need a bicycle so I can ride with my friends."

"I am sorry, son," said his Dad. "We are starting a new business and we need all our money to make it work. We just can't afford it now—maybe for your birthday in February."

Austin looked sad but said, "Thanks."

Adventure #2

Austin's cousin Julio came over to visit on Tuesday. He rode his super-speed racing bike. Julio demonstrated riding on the back wheel all the way up the sidewalk. He told Austin to try it.

Austin said, "I don't have a bicycle. I will get one for my birthday."

Julio thought about it and said, "Here, try mine."

Austin worked hard at getting the bike to stay on the back wheel. He almost had it when Julio said it was time for him to go home.

Julio was almost at the end of the sidewalk when he turned around and came back. "Hey Austin," he said, "Would you like to borrow my bicycle this week while I am away at camp?"

"Sure," said Austin.

"Okay, let's walk it to my house. Then you can ride it home."

Austin rode the bicycle back to his house. He felt like the wind was carrying him. He rode all afternoon.

Later that evening, Julio walked up to Austin. "I'm sorry, but the trip to camp has been canceled because of flooding. I need my bike back."

Austin was sad, but he handed the bike over to Julio and said, "Thank you for letting me have it for the day."

©Teacher Created Resources, Inc.

Chapter 7   Story Writing

Story Writing (cont.)

Class Guided Writing: Austin's Bicycle (cont.)

Step 2: Package (cont.)

Middle (cont.)

Adventure #3

Isabel came over the next day with a plastic bag on her handlebars. She had a sprocket chain and pedals.

"Here, I brought you some bicycle parts. Maybe you could build your own."

"Thanks," Austin looked at the parts. He remembered some more parts in the garage.

Soon all his friends were finding parts for him. He got out some tools and tried to put bicycle parts together. He tried and tried. His friends tried. The parts just did not fit, no matter how hard he tried. Austin was sad, but he said thank you to all his friends.

Ending

Solution

Mom called Austin in from sitting under the tree. She said, "Mrs. Kimmel across the street wants her lawn mowed. She can pay $5. If you mow lawns and do some work around the neighborhood, you could save enough money to buy a new bicycle. You will be proud of something you earned yourself. Here is a jar for your money."

"Sounds like a plan!" exclaimed Austin.

Austin went to Mrs. Kimmel's house and asked if he could have the job of mowing her lawn. Mrs. Kimmel smiled and nodded her head yes.

The work was hard. He could smell the cut grass. Later, Mrs. Kimmel brought out tangy lemonade and told him to take a break. Austin had never worked for anyone before, but it felt good.

The next day, Mrs. Kline wanted her flower garden weeded. She paid $2.

That evening, Mr. Alvera wanted his yard raked. He paid $3.

In no time at all, the neighbors knew that Austin would do odd jobs and work hard. He earned enough money that month for a small bicycle. He looked at the sale paper for bicycles. He and Dad decided it would be better to earn more money and buy a bigger bike because he was growing. He worked a little longer and soon bought a racing bike like Julio's.

Epilog

Later that summer, Austin wanted a T-shirt with his favorite team logo on the front. He knew exactly how to get it. He asked in the neighborhood if anyone had any odd jobs. Soon he was wearing his new shirt.

Steps 3 and 4: Pop and Polish

After completing Steps 1 and 2 (Plan and Package), the students will be ready to revise and edit (Pop and Polish) the class story as a group.

Step 5: Publish

Help the students decide how they would like to publish the class story.

Chapter 7   *Story Writing*

Name _____   **Date** _____

Story Planner

Beginning

1. Problem

3. Characters

4. Setting

Middle

5. Adventure

A. _____

B. _____

Ending

2. Solution

6. Happily Ever After

Chapter 7   Story Writing

Name _____   Date _____

Story Planner (cont.)

_____
Story Title

Beginning (introduces characters, setting, and problem)

_____
_____
_____
_____
_____

Middle (adventures to attempt to solve the problem)

_____
_____
_____
_____
_____
_____

Ending (how character(s) solved the problem and Epilog)

_____
_____
_____
_____
_____

A. **Pop** words or ideas in, out, or around.

B. Hold a peer or teacher conference to **polish** your writing.

C. Finally, write a neat draft to **publish** your work.

Chapter 7 *Story Writing*

Name _____ **Date** _____

_____
Story Title

Chapter 7 — Story Writing

Ideas for Story Writing

Personal Experiences

new friend
old friend
best friend
first day of school
weekend activities
hobbies
fondest memory
memorable dream

Animals

endangered animals
zoo animals
jungle animals
desert animals
forest animals
arctic animals

Letters

to an ancestor
to a pen pal
to the newspaper
to the principal
to a person in history
to a book author
to a grandparent
to my hero or heroine

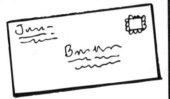

If I Could Be . . .

invisible
famous
an explorer
a pilot
a U.S. president
a doctor
a teacher
a police officer
an author
a king or queen

Favorites

day of the year
secret place
singer
TV show
place to go
breakfast
snack
movie
game
season
activity
book

Books

book for a younger person
sequel to familiar story
Animal ABCs
Famous People ABCs
Food ABCs
drama
biography
autobiography
mystery
picture book
joke book
comic book